Disney Solos
FOR F HORN

MW01206345

Note to Performer: Some melodic phrases have octave adjustments to accommodate your instrument.

ISBN 0-634-00071-3

Wonderland Music Company, Inc.
Walt Disney Music Company

DISTRIBUTED BY

HAL•LEONARD®
CORPORATION

7777 W. BLUEMOUND RD. P.O. BOX 13819 MILWAUKEE, WI 53213

Visit Hal Leonard Online at
www.halleonard.com

BE OUR GUEST
from Walt Disney's BEAUTY AND THE BEAST

Lyrics by HOWARD ASHMAN
Music by ALAN MENKEN

F HORN

THE BELLS OF NOTRE DAME

from Walt Disney's THE HUNCHBACK OF NOTRE DAME

Music by ALAN MENKEN
Lyrics by STEPHEN SCHWARTZ

CD
◆**3** : With melody cue
◆**4** : Accompaniment only

F HORN

CAN YOU FEEL THE LOVE TONIGHT

from Walt Disney Pictures' THE LION KING

Music by ELTON JOHN
Lyrics by TIM RICE

F HORN

I JUST CAN'T WAIT TO BE KING

from Walt Disney Pictures' THE LION KING

Music by ELTON JOHN
Lyrics by TIM RICE

F HORN

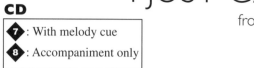

COLORS OF THE WIND

from Walt Disney's POCAHONTAS

Music by ALAN MENKEN
Lyrics by STEPHEN SCHWARTZ

F HORN

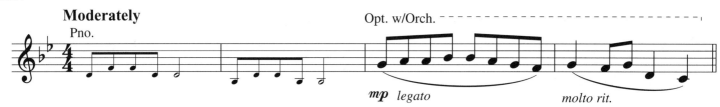

FRIEND LIKE ME

from Walt Disney's ALADDIN

Lyrics by HOWARD ASHMAN
Music by ALAN MENKEN

F HORN

PART OF YOUR WORLD

from Walt Disney's THE LITTLE MERMAID

Lyrics by HOWARD ASHMAN
Music by ALAN MENKEN

F HORN

Pop Ballad

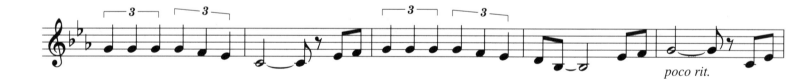

UNDER THE SEA
from Walt Disney's THE LITTLE MERMAID

Lyrics by HOWARD ASHMAN
Music by ALAN MENKEN

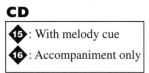

F HORN

REFLECTION
(Pop Version)
from Walt Disney Pictures' MULAN

Music by MATTHEW WILDER
Lyrics by DAVID ZIPPEL

CD

17 : With melody cue
18 : Accompaniment only

F HORN

YOU'LL BE IN MY HEART

(Pop Version)

from Walt Disney Pictures' TARZAN™

Words and Music by
PHIL COLLINS

F HORN

YOU'VE GOT A FRIEND IN ME

from Walt Disney's TOY STORY

Music and Lyrics by
RANDY NEWMAN

F HORN

CD

23 : With melody cue
24 : Accompaniment only

ZERO TO HERO

from Walt Disney Pictures' HERCULES

Music by ALAN MENKEN
Lyrics by DAVID ZIPPEL

F HORN

Much faster "a la Baptist Church"

Sax *Solo*